Lost in Blunderland
The further adventures of Clara

"Aunt Sarum has handed the business to me" (*Page 26*)

Lost in Blunderland
The further adventures of Clara

A political parody based on
Lewis Carroll's Wonderland

by Caroline Lewis

ILLUSTRATIONS BY
J. STAFFORD RANSOME

2010

Published by Evertype, Cnoc Sceichín, Leac an Anfa, Cathair na Mart, Co. Mhaigh Eo, Éire. *www.evertype.com*.

This edition © 2010 Michael Everson.

First edition London: William Heinemann, 1903.

All rights reserved. No part of this publication may be reproduced, stored in a retrieval system, or transmitted, in any form or by any means, electronic, mechanical, photocopying, recording, or otherwise, without the prior permission in writing of the Publisher, or as expressly permitted by law, or under terms agreed with the appropriate reprographics rights organization.

A catalogue record for this book is available from the British Library.

ISBN-10 1-904808-50-6
ISBN-13 978-1-904808-50-3

Typeset in De Vinne Text, Mona Lisa, ENGRAVERS' ROMAN, and *Liberty* by Michael Everson.

Illustrations: J. Stafford Ransome, 1903.

Cover: Michael Everson.

Printed by LightningSource.

Foreword

Clara in Blunderland was written in 1902 and details the adventures of Arthur Balfour while being groomed to become Prime Minister—the Clara of *Lost in Blunderland*, published in 1903, is Balfour once he got the job. The two novels deal with British frustration and anger about the Boer War and with Britain's political leadership at the time.

Caroline Lewis is a pen-name, that of the team of Edward Harold Begbie (1871–1929), J. Stafford Ransome (born 1860), and M. H. Temple. Much of Begbie's work was as a journalist, though he also wrote non-fiction, biographies, and some twenty-five novels, ranging from children's stories to explorations of personal psychology and spirituality. He wrote some of his best-known investigative and satirical work under the pen-name "A Gentleman with a Duster".

J. Stafford Ransome, the illustrator of both *Blunderland* books, also worked as a journalist. Moreover he wrote on such wide-ranging subjects as labour relations, engineering in South Africa, and woodworking machinery.

In 1902 M. H. Temple collaborated again with Begbie and Ransome in *The Coronation Nonsense Book* (in the style of

Edward Lear). In 1894 he contributed satirical political verse to *The Hawarden Horace* by Charles L. Graves.

Caroline Lewis' jokes and allusions are too rich and densely woven into this book to explain them all—more a theme for an academic thesis than for a foreword like this, and I am no expert in any case. But I can supply a few biographical summaries (to 1903) and photos to assist the reader to put the cartoon parodies into context, and guide the reader who wishes to pursue an interest in any of these characters, or in the particulars of Balfour's early premiership.

Clara: Arthur Balfour (1848–1930) was Prime Minister of the United Kingdom from 1902 to 1905. He came into power at about the same time as the coronation of Edward VII and the end of the South African War. *Lost in Blunderland* was written *after* Balfour became Prime Minister in 1902 on Lord Salisbury's resignation.

The Red Queen: Joseph Chamberlain (1836–1914) was Secretary of State for the Colonies from 1895 to 1903. In 1899, with British public opinion in favour of military support for the "Uitlanders", he pressed for troop reinforcements to be sent to South Africa. As a result the Boer republics of the Transvaal and the Orange Free State declared war on Great Britain.

The White Knight: St John Brodrick, 1st Earl of Midleton (1856–1942), Conservative Member of Parliament for Guildford, was Secretary of State for War from 1900 to 1903.

The Duchess ("Aunt Sarum"): Robert Cecil, 3rd Marquess of Salisbury (1830–1903) was Prime Minister from 1895 to 1902, serving as Foreign Secretary at the same time. Arthur Balfour was his nephew. The Fashoda crisis occurred during his premiership, and more importantly the Second Boer War (1899–1902). (*Sarum* was the ecclesiastical name of the diocese of Salisbury from the 11th century to the Reformation.)

Crumpty-Bumpty, White Queen: Sir Henry Campbell-Bannerman (1836–1908) became leader of the Liberals in the House of Commons in 1898. The Boer War (1899–1902) had split the Liberal party into Imperialist and Pro-Boer camps and the party was defeated in the "khaki election" of 1900.

The Dalmeny Cat, The White King: Archibald Philip Primrose, 5th Earl of Rosebery (1847–1929) was Prime Minister from 1894 to 1895. He was in favour of the Boer War and was against Home Rule for Ireland. His opposition to this latter policy meant that he could not participate in the Liberal Government of 1905.

The Black Knight: Michael Hicks Beach, 1st Earl St Aldwyn (1837– 1916) was known as "Black Michael", and served as Chancellor of the Exchequer from 1885 to 1886 and again from 1895 to 1902. When Lord Salisbury retired in 1902, Hicks Beach also left the government.

The Jugged Rabbit: Edmund Barton (1849–1920) was an Australian politician and judge, who was elected the first Prime Minister of Australia in 1901. In 1903 he resigned from the position of Prime Minister of Australia to become a judge of Australia's High Court.

The Sprigg Chicken: Sir Gordon Sprigg (1830-1913) was four-time Prime Minister of the Cape Colony.

The New Zealand Mutton: Richard Seddon (1845–1906) served as Prime Minister of New Zealand from 1893 to 1906. He had been a strong supporter of the Second Boer War and of preferential trade between British colonies, and believed that New Zealand should play a major role in the Pacific Islands as a "Britain of the South".

But you don't need to be an expert in early twentieth-century British politics to enjoy either book—the story's parody of Lewis Carroll's *Wonderland* books is still fresh and funny even more than a century later. Politics and politicians haven't changed much, it seems, in a century. That may be regrettable—but at least Caroline Lewis can still make us laugh about it!

Michael Everson
Westport 2010

Dedication to the 1903 Edition

With profound apologies
to the
numberless admirers
of the incomparable work of
Lewis Carroll and Sir John Tenniel
this parody is
dedicated
to that framer of our
destinies
THE MAN IN THE STREET

Preface to the 1903 edition

The sole object of the following book is to elucidate those obscure passages in *Clara in Blunderland* which have convulsed the Chancelleries of Europe.

Persons of a prying habit of mind have persisted in tracing political allusions in the innocent if not lucid narrative of Clara's former adventures. The Author and the Artist beg to be allowed to disclaim anything of the sort. The one, as the reader may easily ascertain for himself, is totally ignorant of all politics whatsoever; and the other is, for reasons unnecessary to mention, entirely incapable of a portrait which the mother of the patient would recognize.

All the obscurities of the earlier book are cleared up in this. For instance, the Dalmeny Cat is shown to be really the White King; the hatching of Crumpty-Bumpty is expanded and explained; the identity of the White Knight, whom some have confounded with the Rt. Hon. St John Brodrick, is made clear; the Red Queen is the Red Queen, and no one else; and everything, either in the text or the illustrations, which could be twisted into the suggestion of a likeness between Clara and our illustrious Prime Minister has been carefully expunged.

The Author and the Artist hold totally divergent views on practically every subject touched upon in either book, and are agreed only in desiring to place it upon record, that the Unicorn is merely a fabulous monster.

Trusting that this clear explanation will set at rest all misapprehensions, they leave this work to the judgment of a discerning public.

Blunderland, S.W.
32 July 1903

Lost in Blunderland
The further adventures of Clara

Contents

I. Making Hay *7*
II. Shopping *11*
III. In the Swim *18*
IV. All Smoke *26*
V. Fawning *35*
VI. Hedging and Ditching *43*
VII. Playing with Fire *49*
VIII. Pudding and Pugilists *59*
IX. Hatched Out *65*
X. Under the Peer Tree *73*
XI. A Tight Place *79*
XII. The Picnic *91*
XIII. Shaken *100*
XIV. Taken *102*

THE TANGLED MAZE

Child of the pensive deadwall brow
  And languid eyes, I wonder
How long a time 'twill be ere thou
  Wilt drive us all asunder!
Thy methods, dear, can hardly fail
To rend from head the Tory tail.

Oft have we marked thy listless pose,
  And seen thee fail and falter.
The time must come, how soon, who knows?
  When things will have to alter.
Sufficient let it be to say,
"A dog can only have his day."

O woeful fate! to force on one,
   So eminently suited
In cloistered shades the world to shun,
   These politics polluted.
Better for thee to mount thy car,
And leave the madding crowd afar.

A legacy from other days
   When life was slow and easy,
For thee too tangled is the maze,
   The greasy pole too greasy.
Essay to climb? Thou canst not stand
Apart from Joe's retaining hand!

Come, hearken then, ere public voice,
   With scornful accents laden,
Shall spurn thine Uncle's far-fetched choice,
   O! vacillating maiden!
Ere Britain rises in her ire,
And speaks the fatal word, "Retire".

Fain would we hope 'twere not too late
   For this, our simple story,
To point thee to the golden gate
   Of re-established glory.
Alack a day! We sadly fear
That politics are not thy sphere.

Chapter I

Making Hay

The afternoon was dull and nearly as hot as usual when Clara sat down by her Aunt Sarum in the hayfield.

Close to Aunt Sarum lay heaps and heaps of heavy volumes labelled "Publisher's Returns", and one of them was on her lap.

Aunt Sarum looked very worried, and she glanced continually from the book to a paper of questions, which seemed to cause her a great deal of annoyance

"I ca'n't make it out at all," she said, crossly. "Why *does* a miller wear a white hat?" she muttered to herself. "I don't know. I've read the article 'Hat', and it gives 'Panama'. That's too far-fetched. Then the article on 'White' refers me to 'Ladysmith'. As if I hadn't had enough of South Africa! Let's look up 'Miller'."

"M—a, M—e, M—i, M—i—l, Miller. What's this? What does it say? 'Miller (see Joe)'. See Joe! JOE, indeed! Not if *I* know it."

Aunt Sarum yawned. "Clara, I'm tired of it all—I'm going to give it up. Here, you take the book—you are old enough now to solve the problems of the *Times* for yourself. Take it away—I've done with it, and I don't want to see it any more."

Clara had been watching the men tossing about the hay in the corner of the field, and thought how nice it would be to go over there and help them; for, you see, she could make hay of anything.

However, she obediently lifted the odd volume her Aunt had been reading and tried to understand some of the long words. But there didn't seem to be anything in it about competitions, and very little about golf or motoring. "And what," she said to herself, "is the good of a book that says nothing about bogies and hooting things, and that doesn't even report the proceedings of the Basingstoke Bench?"

Thinking about books and the *Times* and things like that always made Clara's head ache; and this afternoon, whether it was the heat or hay-fever, she began to get drowsy.

Clara could never be quite certain whether she went to sleep or came awake just then.

"You see," she told Geraldine, when they were talking it over in the nursery afterwards, "if I'm asleep now, I was awake then; but if I'm awake now, I must have been asleep then, or *vivâ voce*, or something

"I don't think, my dear, it matters at all which," replied Geraldine sympathetically.

All Clara could remember distinctly was that the hay on which she was sitting suddenly began to shake itself, and heave like an earthquake, and she found herself shooting up like a rocket. A farm labourer had pounced upon the hay and tossed it into the air with his fork.

When Clara came down again, Aunt Sarum had vanished, and so had the volumes.

Gradually a strange feeling came over her, a sort of tickling of the soles of the feet, and swelling of the head. It was a sensation which she had felt before, and she guessed that she was once again in Blunderland.

It was quite true. The old curiousness was coming back. Clara had often felt too big for her boots, but now she felt too big for anything. Her hat especially seemed so uncomfortably tight that she began to be afraid that she must have got the mugwumps, or balkans on the brain.

When she put up her hand she felt a cold hard substance, not at all like the nice little Tam O'Shanter to which she was accustomed. With difficulty she removed it. "Curiouser and curiouser! Why it is a *real* GOLDEN CROWN!" she exclaimed.

You see, it looked like gold, and it was very heavy and dazzling. But Clara, of course, had been taught that all is not gold that comes from Hatfield.

"It's rather hollow," she sighed, "but at all events it didn't come out of a cracker, and they ca'n't say I'm not a real Queen now."

"How wobbly it is!" she said, trying it on again, for she found it difficult to balance. "But perhaps if I can manage to walk quite straight it will keep on, and people wo'n't notice that it wasn't made for me."

Chapter II

Shopping

Clara rubbed her eyes, and looked again. There was no doubt about it, she was in a curious sort of a shop which was full of dust.

And was that really an old Goat on the other side of the counter? Rub as she would, she could make nothing else of it. She was in an old-fashioned shop, leaning with her elbows on the counter, and staring almost rudely at a poor old creature who was sitting placidly pulling at a lot of wires. These wires made some jumping jacks in the window dance about in a funny way. There was one of them, however, that Clara thought looked rather like the Red Queen, which refused to work when the wires pulled its leg.

"Some people would say you were pitch-forked in here," said the creature, with a sneer. "But they would be wrong. You were a Foregone Conclusion. That's what you were, and that's all about it."

"I'm a Queen," said Clara indignantly. "How dare you call me names like that? It's not ladylike." However, she thought it was of no use to be angry, so she asked timidly, "Would you mind telling me whether you are a Goat or a Sheep? You see you wear such queer clothes, and your voice is rather husky."

"I'm an old Conservative Party," said the Goat sulkily, "and I'm feeling quite worn out."

"May I pull those wires for you then?" said Clara, for she was a very polite child, and still liked playing with dolls and things.

"All in good time, all in good time, my dear. You were sent here to do that, and you'll have plenty of wire-pulling before long if they keep you in the shop."

Shopping

"Who's going to keep Me?" said Clara, with her favourite toss of the head. "I'm a Queen, and can keep myself."

"The Constituent, my dear, if you behave yourself; and perhaps if you don't. That is," it added, with a twitch of the lip which showed how few teeth it had left, "that is if you learn how to get round him. You'll see him soon enough. He's like a rabbit—always running away. Put some salt on his tail if you can get near enough."

Clara thought this must be good advice, for her Aunt had often told her to take everything with a grain of salt.

"Now," said the Goat, "what are you going to buy? That's the question of the day."

"Well," said Clara, taken aback, "I should like to look all round me first."

"You may look on both sides of you if you like," said the Goat, "but I don't advise you to look in front or behind. A politician ca'n't afford to look back, and it's against *all* the traditions of *this* shop for anybody to look ahead. We NEVER do that. The best thing you can do is to shut your eyes to almost everything here."

Clara thought she had never before seen so strange a lot of things in a shop.

"What is that palm oil for?" she asked.

"Just now it's mostly used for Indian Princes, and Governors of Portuguese South Africa, but in the good old days there was a great demand for it at election times. Now we use these eggs."

"How much does palm oil cost?"

"It costs *me* a great deal, but I always give it away with slices of territory."

"Then you ca'n't make much profit out of it," said Clara.

"That's all you know," retorted the Goat with a blink. "It's very useful stuff, I can tell you."

"I should like to have a great big watch like that," said Clara, pointing to one that was hanging up.

"It would be of no use to you," said the Goat. "You can lose enough time without that. That's a stop-watch, and we keep those for our Ministers in Pekin."

"Whatever for?" asked Clara.

"So that they shall stop watching of course. But you don't seem to know much," continued the Goat. "I think I'd better tell you what all these things are for. Soft soap we keep for German Emperors, and butter for Afrikander Bondsmen. The Noah's Ark is my own, though I'll let you play with it sometimes. Red tape we wrap ourselves up in. You see, it's more impenetrable than barbed wire. The stickphast I have laid in especially for you. It's Office glue, and you'll want as much as you can get if you are to stop here long. If you don't know how to use it ask Sir Gordon Sprigg. White-led soldiers I prefer to stock, rather than the other sort. They come so much cheaper. Why, in Africa the other day I only paid one and threepence a day for them when I was giving three shillings for black ones."

"*Did* we have any black soldiers in South Africa?" asked Clara, who was rather shocked at the idea.

"It's been officially denied," said the Goat. "What more proof do you want?"

"But don't you keep anything for the public?" asked Clara, by way of changing the conversation.

"Of course I do," said the Goat. "Ca'n't you see the jumbles, and crackers, and gilded pills, and surprise-packets? Those are the things I treat them to."

"But if you *treat* people to everything how do you make your shop pay?" asked Clara, who knew all about domestic economy from her copy-book.

"It doesn't pay," said the Goat, "only you mustn't tell anybody. It used to, years and years ago, before you were born, but it wants a new signboard and floor, repainting outside and in, a new stock throughout, and all sorts of things. I'm too old to bother about it, though, myself," and the Goat seemed all but collapsing.

Clara felt very sorry, but she did not see how she could help the poor creature, and so she went on with her inspection of the shop.

"What's the use of the patchwork?" said she. "It isn't very pretty."

"It's not pretty, perhaps," said the Goat, "but, applied artistically, it's very, very useful. I'm a great believer in it, and use it constantly. No respectable shop of this kind could possibly get on without it.

"But," continued the Goat, "you're a long time making up your mind. *What* do you want to buy?"

Clara was quite bewildered at the number of things in the shop, and could not decide what it was she wanted, or whether she wanted anything at all. And besides, the things seemed to flow about so she never could manage to make out exactly what they were.

There was one bright thing which took her fancy very much, and which she determined to get a steady look at if she possibly could. The Goat said it was a fiscal something, and rather shop-soiled, as it had been in stock for years. Clara said that she thought she would like to play with it a little.

The Goat sniffed. "Of course you can have it if you can get hold of it. But I don't think you're quite old enough to be trusted with it just yet; besides, it's very expensive."

"Oh, I don't mind that a bit," Clara remarked cheerfully (dream money is always more plentiful than the real kind); "but it keeps on changing its shape. It's so confusing."

"Well, I really wish you'd make up your mind," said the Goat, crossly. "It makes me giddy to see you spinning round and round like a factotum, and it's not good for an old Party like me. What you want is a couple of those Education tabloids. They're the very best kind, my dear," said the Goat. "Hugh-Cecil made, and sweetened throughout with our patent Kenyon-Slaney saccharine. Only, if you take one you must take two—we only sell 'em in pairs."

"But I don't think I want two,' said Clara, thinking to herself that one was *quite* as much as good, kind Dr Clifford, who attended to all the family, would allow.

"I ca'n't help that," retorted the Goat. "You must pay for both anyway, and you must take both. It's a rule of our House, and I ca'n't have rules broken just to please a Foregone Conclusion like you."

"But suppose I don't like the first one and it disagrees with me?" asked Clara, who was a very prudent child.

"It'll do that," said the Goat, promptly, "and you'll have to follow it with the passive resistance treatment; but you'll feel better afterwards. You're too plethoric, you know, and there's nothing like it for reducing one."

Clara didn't know what "plethoric" meant, but she thought it must have something to do with big majorities.

"Now, the proper way," the Goat continued, to reduce yourself with these tabloids is to swallow them with your eyes shut as tight as possible, and then to go immediately to the country. That'll reduce you quickly enough."

Clara, like her Aunt Sarum, was always fond of quack remedies, so she did as she was told and swallowed the tabloids.

They were very nasty, and tasted like a mixture of Board Schools, County Councils, and Curates; but she, got them down at last.

Then a most curious thing happened. No sooner had she swallowed the drugs than everything seemed to go round and round, and she found herself swimming about in a great pool of water. The Goat and the shop and everything else had disappeared, and she realized at once that she was quite at sea.

Chapter III

In the Swim

This did not frighten Clara nearly as much as it would have frightened any other little girl, because she kept up her spirits by thinking how buoyant she was, and how many of her relations and friends had been in the same predicament and had come out all right. "Aunt Sarum's been at sea often enough, I'm sure," she said to herself, "and Geraldine's never been anywhere else as long as I can remember. Hughie lives in water a great deal hotter than this, and I never knew the time when Cousin Cranborne wasn't out of his depth either at home or abroad."

Clara had always liked drifting, and it was no new sensation to her not to know in what direction she was being carried; so she just floated on the ebbing tide without making the least effort to swim against it, and made up her mind to enjoy the scenery as she was carried along.

How it happened she never could tell, but suddenly the water round her was filled with all kinds of queer creatures, some of which she recognized at once. For instance, she could not mistake the Dodo, though the poor thing was floating upside-down because its feet were covered with corns. Whenever it could get right side up for a minute or two it kept shouting for somebody to put a tax upon them.

One of the guinea-pigs swam up to Clara just as the Dodo turned over for the fifth time and said it was a bad day for hay-fishers.

"Whatever do you want to talk about such ridiculous things as that for in the middle of an accident?" Clara said very crossly. "I wish you'd go away if you ca'n't be sensible." And the poor guinea-pig dived under water, and she lost sight of it altogether.

"I'm rather sorry I spoke to it like that," said Clara to herself; "but after all, it doesn't much matter. There are plenty more of that kind. Why, at home the woods are full of them. It was a very common sort of guinea-pig, after all."

At this point the other guinea-pig, which had been watching the movements of the first with great attention, remarked that nobody seemed to want a whit more and swam away as hard as it could to the London County Council, where it hid itself in the robes of an Alderman, and died in the odour of London

Municipal Sanctity. "Come," said Clara, "that finishes the guinea-pigs." (But it didn't.) "Now we shall get on better."

In a stagnant backwater Clara came across her old friends the Walrus and the Carpenter. They refused to come over to her, though she called to them, because, as they both said, she seemed to make no progress. Clara couldn't see that they made much themselves, because they only swam round and round one another, like the Double Stars of which she had read. All the time the Carpenter kept explaining to the Walrus that it was the greatest of all beasts—"Which *I* thought rather rude of him," said Clara afterwards, "but the Walrus didn't seem offended"—while the Walrus never ceased telling the Carpenter that he was the only really "Honest" man it had ever seen. But the other creatures only laughed at them, and even the Welsh Stoat, which used to be content with their leavings, declared they were behind the times.

"But they're not," said Clara indignantly. "It's quite impossible for anybody to be behind the *Times* at the present day."

"Have you ever noticed," shouted the Red Queen, "how I kill rats and ferrets?" She was standing on the bank, and when the Stoat caught sight of her it swam away as fast as ever it could, muttering something about "dirty tricks", and the "necessity of protecting British vermin", which Clara could not quite understand.

"It's an idea of my own," the Red Queen went on in a fiercer tone. "I make them eat their own words. Invariably fatal, I find it."

"Well, you manage to eat plenty of your own at times," barked the Irish Terrier, which had been making the most tremendous noise ever since the accident began. "Ssh!" whispered the Secretary Bird. "Remember Land Purchase!" and instantly the Terrier barked itself entirely inside out and turned into a most amiable Pug.

In the Swim

"That's the most curious thing yet," said Clara. "I never saw such a change in all my life. Why, you might almost think it was a Bull-dog now."

Floating near and drifting like herself with the tide, only being in a backwater he went in a contrary direction, Clara saw her old friend Crumpty-Bumpty; but she had scarcely any time to speak to him except just to ask him how many great falls he'd had lately. To this he only gave a melancholy shake of the head, and went rolling on his course to nowhere in particular.

All this time the Red Queen was getting more and more fidgety, and was walking backwards and forwards on the bank. "That child will be the death of me one of these days," she kept on muttering to herself. "Why doesn't her Aunt come back and take care of her? They seem to expect me to nurse the whole family for nothing. It would serve her right if she got drowned or swallowed up by those beasts! Well, I suppose I had better pull her out of it this time. But who's going to look after her when I go on my journey, I should like to know!"

"Here!" shouted the Red Queen to Clara, who was just sinking for the thirteenth time.

"Catch this, you foolish child, and I'll pull you into your depth again." As she spoke, she threw a rope towards Clara, who was just able by taking hold of it to get out of the water and into the mud.

"There you may stick for the present, my dear," said the Queen, rather heartlessly. "It will keep you out of mischief while I'm away." But somehow or other Clara managed to scramble on shore and found that all the creatures were already there, and were looking as if they expected her. When they saw that she had been rescued, they raised a loud cheer. A Rabbit, who was decked out in a splendid heraldic livery, with Clara's coat-of-arms on his pinafore, came to her and introduced himself as the Constituent, and her Herald. He then jumped on to a tub and began to proclaim her style and title as Queen of Blunderland.

"What a nice useful person; I'm sure he doesn't look as if he were going to run away," said Clara. "I think the Goat must be what the papers call an alarmist."

"Hail! Clara Regina!" he shouted, and blew on a little tin trumpet which he had bought on Mafeking Day.

"What *shall* I do?" said Clara, who felt very nervous. "What shall I say to all these—these things?"

"Don't be afraid, your Majesty," said the Constituent. "I'll show you how to do it. You see, I represent popular opinion. To some extent I am responsible for your being here, though it wasn't exactly I who had you crowned. I have always had a liking for your family, and I'll be your Herald, and stick to you through thick and thin. But," he added, with a sort of deferential anxiety, "you mustn't let it be too thin or I shall dwindle away."

"What a noise the animals are making!" said Clara, putting her hands to her ears.

"Come, come, your Majesty," said the Constituent, "this will never do. You must talk to them—make a neat speech."

"I'm sure I don't know what to say to these creatures," Clara whispered. "I ca'n't be expected to please them all."

But still she determined to do her best, though all she could manage to stammer out was, "I am quite a child in these matters."

Immediately the Constituent, whose manner towards her was becoming quite fatherly, blew his trumpet again: and though Clara said nothing herself; and felt all the time as if she were in a dream, the notes sounded like a voice, and seemed to chant the following words:—

> *To the Blunderland creatures 'twas Clara who spoke,*
> *"Now I trust you'll not think me a pig in a poke.*
> *The Red Queen wo'n't have you, you wo'n't have C.-B.,*
> *So Aunt Sarum has handed the business to me.*
>
> *"I'll keep up traditions as well as I can,*
> *Though I look like a child, I'm as strong as a man,*
> *Which is lucky; for Auntie has left unto me*
> *The redemption of promises thirty-times-three!"*

Then all the creatures began to cheer except those on the extreme left, who only laughed and looked scornful. Those near Clara at once began to sing the chorus, but they did not get the words right:—

> *Come, place us in billets as fat as you can,*
> *And we will stand by you—we will, to a man.*
> *You must treat us like Sarums, and then, don't you see,*
> *We will keep you in office till thirty-times-three!*

"Thirty-times-three," thought Clara, making a calculation in her head. "Why, that makes ninety. What an old lady I shall be! It would be rather nice to be a Queen all that time.

"But what do they mean by saying that they want me to treat them as Sarums?" she asked.

"Sarums are artists," said the Constituent, "and you're one yourself."

"Am I?" said Clara. "But I ca'n't draw anything."

"Oh! Yes, you can, my dear," said the Constituent. "You can draw as nicely as any of them."

"What *do* they draw?" asked Clara.

"Salaries," replied the Constituent promptly.

"How very interesting!" said Clara. "And what do they draw upon?"

"Their imaginations, mostly," said the Constituent.

By this time the creatures were getting very impatient. The animals were beginning to growl and the birds to hoot and scream. The Walrus ground his tusks with rage, but the British Lion merely yawned lazily.

"Talk to them, my dear," whispered the Constituent. "Say something, promise them everything they ask for, or they'll tear you to pieces."

"I wo'n't," said Clara, decidedly, with a stamp of the foot. "I'm a Queen, and I shall let them see that I can govern them all by myself. I'm not going to be bullied, so I shall tell them what I think."

The Constituent sounded his tin trumpet again until the noise ceased a little; and then Clara, who was really feeling more nervous than ever, proceeded with her speech. This time she said the words herself:—

> *Now, Blunderland creatures, I tell you! Draw near.*
> *I shall do as I like and I wish to make clear,*
> *That Dizzy, and Pam. and the late Mr G.,*
> *All rolled into one would be miles behind me.*
>
> *So put on rose glasses and live upon hope,*
> *I'll lather you daily with softest of soap.*
> *From me you'll get always more halfpence than kicks,*
> *So keep me in Office till sixty-times-six!*

At this all the creatures grew extremely angry, and with a yell they changed the tone of their chorus:—

She fills up her speeches with bombast and bluff,
We really have had far too much of such stuff.
Sling mud by the handful; submerge her in brine,
And don't let her up till she's ninety-tines-nine!

Then there was a terrible clamour, and all the creatures looked so fierce that Clara hid her face.

"Come along, you silly child," said a voice at her elbow, and some one seized her hand. Turning round Clara saw it was the Red Queen, who had been standing quietly by, looking on at the strange doings.

"Come along away from them all; you'll be eaten up. I know you will. Your Aunt Sarum was trouble enough, but at all events she sat still a good deal. But you, you take yourself seriously, and that will never do."

All this time the Constituent was bustling about, shaking hands with all the creatures near him.

"What a moral victory! What a splendid moral victory!" he kept saying.

"What is a moral victory?" asked Clara.

"It is a by-election," said the Red Queen, with a scowl. "Now come along, I want to talk to you."

Chapter IV

All Smoke

"And now, Clara, I must leave you for a time," said the Red Queen. "I am going on a long, voyage to Spriggland, where the Porlokrock used to live."

"Oh!" said Clara with a gasp. "Mind they don't eat you up."

"They ca'n't do *that*," said the Red Queen. "I'm too tough."

"What are you going to do there?" said Clara.

"It's no good my telling you that, my dear; you wouldn't understand," said the Red Queen. "How you'll get on without me I really don't know," she continued. "Let me advise you to sit still all the time. I sha'n't be away for long, and when they ask you any questions be sure not to answer 'yes' or 'no'. Say 'I'll see', and then wait for me to come back."

Clara thought her rather patronizing, but as the Red Queen had saved her on so many occasions she did not like to show that it made her cross. So she said nothing.

Then the air became so thick with black smoke that Clara began to feel quite uncomfortable.

"It's nothing," said the Red Queen. "It's only my private man-of-war."

Clara was just able to see through the darkness that they were on the end of a pier and that there was a large ship alongside. All the creatures were assembled there to say goodbye to the Red Queen.

"Take care of yourself my dear," said the Queen as she went on board, "and whatever you do, don't get into mischief."

Clara took out her handkerchief and put it to her eyes. She was not really *very* sorry, but she had always seen people do that at parting.

When she looked up again the ship had already left, and all the creatures were waving their handkerchiefs enthusiastically. The Walrus and the Carpenter, who hated the Red Queen more than all the others, were the most frantic in their joy.

"The pier must have melted away," explained Clara to Geraldine afterwards. So; indeed, must the creatures; all except a Lizard, which Clara had not noticed before, and the Constituent.

The Lizard said it had been on board to see the Red Queen off and had fallen down the, smoke stack, and been blown out again. "I'm always getting blown up somehow," it said with a helpless smile, "but *I* ca'n't help it if I lose my way."

"It comes of poking your nose into things that don't concern you," said the Constituent.

They were standing on a cliff and looking out to sea at the Red Queen's ship, which was now only a tiny speck on the horizon.

"What a terrible lot of smoke!" said Clara.

"Yes," said the Lizard proudly. "That's the smoke from the foreign boilers used in the British Navy. They burn more coal than all the other ships in the world put together."

"Isn't it very expensive?" asked Clara.

"I expect so," said the Lizard. "I expect so, but you see, it's not in my department. That's the Admiralty's invention, and the notion is that if one of our ships were to get up steam the dense cloud of smoke would hide the whole fleet and so none of them could be hit."

"It's rather clever," "admitted Clara, "but what are you?"

"I deal in foreign affairs," said the Lizard, "and now that the Red Queen's gone there's a foreigner, a dear friend of mine, I want to introduce you to. May I go and fetch it?"

"It isn't another beast, I hope?" said Clara with a sigh. You see, she was beginning to feel that she must only be Queen of a sort of Zoological Gardens after all.

"Well, the French call it the *bête noir*," said the Lizard, apologetically. "But it's a very fine creature. It's a Unicorn, and it talks English."

"Does it bite?" asked Clara.

"It usually barks a great deal and always crows," the Lizard; "but it gets no further than that, as a rule."

"Oh, very well," said Clara. "But I'm rather tired. You can go and fetch it while I rest here."

When the Lizard had gone, the Constituent touched Clara on the shoulder. "I wouldn't make its acquaintance if I were your Majesty," he suggested, timidly. "You know what the Red Queen said about getting into mischief. She doesn't think much of foreigners, and she loathes Unicorns."

"You seem to think there's nobody in the world but the Red Queen," said Clara, quite crossly. "Aunt Sarum said I was old enough to do things for myself. I shall see this Unicorn and perhaps get it to advise me instead of you. You're only the man in the street after all, and ca'n't be expected to know much."

The Constituent looked reproachfully at Clara, but said nothing.

And then she sat gazing dreamily at the clouds of smoke which seemed to fill the whole sky.

And as she watched them her childish fancy conjured up the outlines of half-forgotten faces. There was her Aunt Sarum's face, as plain as in real life, and others of people whom she remembered her Aunt had said were once great Queens of Blunderland in their day.

"I suppose I am quite as great a person now as they were," said Clara, half to herself.

"Not yet," said the Constituent, whose voice seemed rather husky.

By degrees the smoke formed itself into a sort of frame, in which the centre grew quite clear. "Just as if there was going to be a magic lantern show," said Clara afterwards.

And then, one after another, pictures gradually appeared and dissolved in the space. They looked like the shadow-pictures you make on the wall.

The first picture was a curious one. The Red Queen was piling papers on a bonfire and holding out her hand for more.

"There she is!" said the Constituent, "persuading the Natalians to burn their claims against Blunderland for damage which they did not sustain by the war. That's a very striking picture, isn't it?"

"But if they weren't real claims, would Blunderland have paid them?" asked Clara.

"Of course it would. That's what it's there for. Ah! That's a masterpiece. It shows how clever the Red Queen is and how loyal the Natalians are." And the Constituent clapped his hands and chuckled.

Then the picture faded, and another took its place.

"That," said the Constituent, "must be the Red Queen at the Rand Mines. And there's the honest miner, I declare, handing over thirty million pounds of his hard-earned sweatings, and promising to lend her thirty-five millions more."

"Isn't he rather a funny-looking miner?" asked Clara.

"Oh, no—not at all. Modern miners are very respectable people, I can assure you. Most of them wear large diamond rings and live in Park Lane," said the Constituent.

"She really must be very clever to get all that money," said Clara.

"She could have got ever so much more if she had only asked for it," said the Constituent, who didn't seem very enthusiastic.

The next picture showed a tall man carrying a very heavy weight up a steep hill, while the Red Queen looked on approvingly.

"Why, there's Lord Milner!" shouted the Constituent joyfully. "What a heavy load he's carrying, and all by himself, too! He was sent out from Blunderland to carry that. The Red Queen seems to be encouraging him, but why doesn't she give him a helping hand?"

"That's *splendid*," said Clara. "I wish somebody would do my lessons for me like that."

"I don't think much of that picture," said the Constituent. "She ought to help him up the hill with that heavy load. She's strong enough, I'm sure, and it's a shame to make him do it all by himself. He's been carrying it up that hill for years, but no one ever helps him."

Then came a picture where the Red Queen was trying to catch an insignificant little creature which was running away as fast as its legs would carry it.

"She's in Cape Colony now, and that's a common or gordon sprigg."

"Why is it trying to hide itself?" asked Clara.

"Because it thinks the Red Queen has come to kill it," said the Constituent, "and I only wish she would."

"I think you're very cruel," said Clara. "But your opinions are not worth much. I don't think she wants to hurt it, only it's so silly and frightened!"

"There you see," she continued triumphantly, as the next picture showed the Queen petting the insect. "I told you so. She must be kind as well as clever."

But the Constituent was tearing his fur out by the claw-full.

"I call it most disgraceful," he said. "She has spoilt the effect of the whole journey. Oh dear! Oh dear!" And he wrung his paws in despair.

There were no more pictures, and the clouds closed in and became thicker than ever.

"Why, it's only ended in smoke after all," cried Clara.

"That's what mostly happens in Blunderland," sulkily replied the Constituent.

Chapter V

Fawning

The scene changed, and Clara found herself sitting under a tree.

Feeling restless, she thought she would like to wander in the wood close by. "A wood is such a nice place for doing nothing in," she said to herself. "And oh! I *would* like to find that dear little Lizard again."

She had not gone far in before she saw sticking out of a ditch two legs encased in white armour.

She was quite used to strange things by this time. Besides, her Aunt Sarum had always told her to take everything for granted.

"You see, my dear," her Aunt had said, "if you never seem surprised, people will think you much more clever than you are, because it will look as if you knew all about it beforehand."

Clara on this occasion, however, could not help an exclamation of surprise.

"Surely I've seen those warlike legs before!" she cried. "It *must* be my old friend the White Knight again—and in his favourite attitude. I expect he's thinking out some wonderful new invention."

She examined the legs carefully before she said anything, for she did not want to make a mistake, and her Aunt Sarum had cautioned her often against; speaking to strangers.

When she saw the letters "W. O." on the knee-straps she knew that she was right, and she was very glad, because she loved this helpless old man with the donkey helmet better than any the other strange creatures she had ever met in Blunderland.

Clara looked round for the patient old Bull which the White Knight used to ride so heavily, but it was nowhere to he seen.

She approached the ditch cautiously. "Are you there?" she said, remembering that at the telephone, when you are not quite sure to whom you are speaking, that's what people say.

"Yes," said the White Knight from the bottom of the ditch. "But don't cut me off, and be sure not to switch me anywhere. Though you might disconnect me if you can. But put me on to—on to—my feet again, there's a good fellow."

Clara thought he was rather offhand in his manner of addressing a Queen, but of course he could not see who she was. With some difficulty she managed to help him out of the ditch."

"What's become of your dear old horse?" said Clara, who always liked patting animals.

"What! Old John Bull?" said the White Knight. "He's left me, I'm afraid for ever." At this he burst into tears.

"Never mind," said Clara, putting her arm round his neck soothingly. "What's the matter? There then, tell me all about it."

"Well," sobbed the White Knight, "first of all he took to jibbing. That didn't matter, because, of course, he only stood still, which is what I always wanted him to do."

"What made him behave like that?" asked Clara.

"He didn't seem to like my latest inventions. He shied at my beautiful army corpses, six of them all laid out, and four as dead as the drill-book; he jibbed at my superior Argentine mutton; and when I invented my improved method of buying remounts on the higher purchase system, he kicked over the traces and bolted. But the best of it is," continued the Knight, brightening up, "he's got to keep me all the same. He ca'n't get out of that just yet."

Clara had long since given up wondering at things, and was not a bit surprised to find that in Blunderland horses kept their masters, "although," as she said to Geraldine afterwards, "I suppose it *was* rather funny."

All this time they were sauntering along, the White Knight on all fours, and Clara with her arm round his neck.

"Why do you walk like that?" asked Clara. "Isn't it rather awkward?"

"Extremely awkward," said the White Knight, "but it's my latest invention."

"What's it for?" asked Clara.

"Well, you see," replied the Knight, "I've fallen so often, and into so many holes, and among so many thieves, and so low, that I never get up now. When I walk like this, of course I ca'n't fall any lower, and I am happy."

"That *is* a wonderful invention," said Clara. "I think I'll practise it myself when I get back to the House."

Clara's curiosity was as great as ever, and she found herself again longing to catch a glimpse of the face of this wonderful person who thought of so many brilliant things.

"Wo'n't you take off your—your helmet?" said Clara. "And let me see you as you really are?"

"No!" said the White Knight, decidedly. "I *never* take that off except when I go to the German Manœuvres. Then I dress myself up as a Colonel of the Guildford Fire Brigade, and they take me for Baden-Powell."

"How nice!" said Clara.

"Yes, and I had my photograph taken, too, like that," said the White Knight, proudly.

"Oh! Wo'n't you give—" began Clara.

Then an accident happened. The White Knight stumbled and his helmet came off in Clara's hand, and she found herself gazing in astonishment on the face of a very ordinary looking man.

"I'm *so* sorry," said Clara, "but I *really* couldn't help it." She was a very conscientious little girl, and wouldn't have done anything so rude on any account of her own free will.

"It doesn't matter," said the White Knight, not at all disconcerted. "And now that we know each other, let us shake hands. You see, we're both in the same boat, you and I."

Clara didn't see any boat at all, but she shook hands quite willingly with him. "What boat?" she asked.

"Well, you see, you're a Foregone Conclusion. I suppose they've told you that," said the Knight.

"Yes, I know," said Clara. "The old Goat said so. But I don't know what it means."

"It means that you were not exactly pitch-forked into the Shop."

"The Goat said that, too," admitted Clara.

"Well," explained the Knight, "*I* was never a Foregone Conclusion, and I *was* pitchforked into these clothes, and they don't fit."

"Then, why don't you get into something else?" asked Clara.

"That's just it," said the Knight. "They're very awkward, but I like them. It's rather useful to have cast-iron clothes, for then you see you ca'n't be pitchforked out of them. Besides, you know, if I were to take them off, perhaps no one would give me any others. That's what worries me."

"But I'm Queen of Blunderland now," said Clara, "and I would tell them to give you some very pretty ones. I'm fond of you, you see," she added kindly, "though I'm sure I don't know why."

The White Knight shook his head sadly, as he put his helmet on again, and tears came into his eyes.

"Thank you, my dear," he said. "I know that you'll do what you can, but I'm afraid that that's not much. You see, the Constituent seems to be growing tired of you already, and without his assistance you ca'n't remain Queen for long.

"I'll tell you what," added the Knight. "You and I will make a compact. We must stick by each other. Shake hands again."

They shook hands, and Clara was very touched at the forlorn appearance of her companion.

"What compact shall we make?" she asked.

"I've got it all written down here," said the Knight, pulling out a roll of official paper, which Clara remembered to have seen before. "Here it is." And he read: "It is hereby agreed that you, of the one part, shall stick to me whatever happens."

"Oh! Yes, I'll do that," said Clara, quite pleased to find that she was of use to somebody. "And what do *you* agree to do?"

"I'm coming to that, and I assure you I undertake a grave responsibility. It is this: 'I, of the other part, agree to cling on to your skirts wherever you go'," read the Knight.

"But supposing you fell down again, you might pull me down too," suggested Clara.

"I have invented an antidote for that," said the Knight. "You must cling on to the Red Queen's skirts just as I shall to yours. It's our only hope."

"But perhaps she wo'n't make a compact with me like that one I have just made with you," said Clara.

"Oh! Yes, she will, if you go the right away about it," said the Knight with conviction. "You must go to her and promise to do everything she tells you with your eyes shut, and then she will take you in hand. She will call you her leader, by which she means a person who says, 'Ditto'. You see you must do everything she tells you, and I will do everything you tell me. But of course," he added, "I must tell you what to tell me. Then we shall be quite safe."

Clara did not like to think that she could not get along by herself. "Oh! I *do* wish," she said, "I had bought some of that Office glue from the Old Goat, instead of those nasty Education Pills."

"Never mind, my dear," said the Knight. "Think of the magic word 'Ditto', and when the Red Queen comes back, go up to her at once and say it. Keep on saying it as fast as you can to her, and nothing else all day long."

"It seems rather a *silly* word," said Clara, more to herself than to any one else.

"So it is, my dear," said the Knight. "Extremely silly. But," he added very solemnly, "it's better than saying something sillier."

"I must remember that word," said Clara; and as they wandered on she kept repeating to herself "Ditto—ditto—ditto—ditto."

Chapter VI

Hedging and Ditching

"Now, if you think you've got that word into your head," said the White Knight, clinging to Clara's skirts, "we'll go on. It's rather an awkward bit of country we're coming to just here, but it will afford an excellent opportunity of testing our compact."

The Knight's description was not at all exaggerated, and Clara found that, when they had got a little further, they were in a slippery sort of swamp, bounded by broad ditches, filled with very dirty water.

"You don't expect me to cross all those, do you?" she asked the Knight. "Why, I can see from here that some of the planks over those ditches are quite rotten, and some of the ditches have got no planks at all. We must find some by-way out of this."

"I ca'n't help the planks being rotten," returned the Knight. "They are the very best we could pick out of our platform, and your Aunt Sarum, who was much heavier than you, managed to get across somehow. But perhaps she's strained them a little."

So they floundered on for some little distance until they came to the first ditch, which Clara saw was labelled "Woolwich". The plank by which they had to cross it looked dreadfully shaky, and she was very much afraid to trust herself upon it. However, the Knight encouraged her by saying, "Be a Queen now, do. Just shut your eyes and take a leap in the dark, and you'll be over before you know where you are."

Clara didn't half like it, for the Knight was dragging heavily on her skirts, but, as she felt she *must* go forward, she shut her eyes, as she had been told, and began to walk the plank.

Unfortunately, her foot slipped in some crooks in the wood. Then the plank broke in two, and she tumbled off into the dirty water below with a little scream. She wasn't a bit hurt really, though at first she thought all her bones were broken by the fall, and the Knight, who still had tight hold of her, and seemed to have made no effort to cross over, quietly pulled her back on to the bank again. She was very wet and dirty, and it took her some time to recover her breath after all the slime and duckweed she had had to swallow. She felt cross with the Knight for not trying to help himself. "I'm sure," she said, "if you'd only jumped a little, and not pulled so hard, we should have got over all right."

"You seem to think, my dear," replied the Knight, without noticing Clara's vexation, "that it's you who have to cling on to me, and not I to you. Why, if it hadn't been for me you'd have been drowned altogether."

"But you've pulled me back to where we started from," said Clara. "That's no good."

"Anyhow, you haven't lost much this time," said the Knight.

"Have I lost anything?" asked Clara anxiously, feeling in her pockets.

"Only a little credit, my dear," said the Knight.

"Oh! That's nothing," said Clara, who was sure she didn't possess anything of that sort.

"Now you're in a better frame of mind," remarked the Knight, "I don't mind telling you why I didn't try and jump. I was afraid of spoiling my clothes. You see, I ca'n't stand ragging. It would never do for *me* to be 'ragged'. They might take me for a real soldier, and then I don't know *what* would happen."

"We must try to get over at some easier place," said Clara, who didn't think this at all interesting, and she dragged the Knight along to a ditch which was at the end of a field of Rye, and had a bridge across it.

This looked so safe that Clara began to cross over it without any hesitation. To her despair it was a great deal worse than the other; "for," as she said in describing what happened, "no sooner had I put my foot upon it than the other end of the nasty thing suddenly rose up in the air and knocked me right over into the water again."

She was really rather hurt this time, and though it was some satisfaction to her to find that she had pulled the Knight in with her, she sat down at the bottom of the ditch and had a good cry.

"Oh, don't take on so!" moaned the poor Knight, wringing out his hair as he spoke. "I always *did* say that Brook-field was a nasty dangerous place. But remember what a great girl you are—don't cry!"

The opposite bank was far too steep for them, so they crawled back as best they could into the field from which they had come.

Clara dried her eyes, and after shaking as much of the water as she could out of her frock, which was getting very draggled indeed by this time, did her best to smile and look as if she didn't really mind it.

"That's a brave girl," said the Knight. "We'll try and find something safer." And almost as he spoke they came upon a way-bridge, which looked quite secure.

"I don't know whether it is or not," replied Clara, "but I'm sure I'm not going to cross it in the same way as the others." Clara said this because she saw a new motor-tricycle standing all by itself in the field, and a happy thought struck her. "You get into the trailer," she said to the Knight, "and we'll make the car jump it."

So they got into the motor together, and Clara, who was a very bold driver and never paid any attention to the legal rate of speed, pulled all the levers at once and set the car full-tilt at the ditch. The White Knight weighed so much with all his armour and things that they very nearly came to grief after all, but the motor just cleared the bank on the opposite side and landed them safely, with a triumphant "Pip-pip!"

Clara had never felt so glad in her life as when they were safely over at last, and she and the White Knight congratulated one another until they were both quite hoarse.

"It was a narrow squeak," he said. "Now," he continued, "you're through the worst of your troubles for the moment, but some day you will have to try and jump the whole lot. There are six hundred and something of them, and if you are not more skilful than this, you will certainly be drowned."

"Do you think the Constituent would help me?" asked Clara.

"He wo'n't help *you* any more," said the Knight. "But if you ca'n't face the ditches, you will have to hedge carefully, that's all."

"What's hedging?" said Clara.

"Why, saying 'Ditto' to the Red Queen, of course," answered the Knight impatiently. "But I must be off now for a bit. I see the Lizard is coming to look after you, and I don't want to meet it just now."

"Why ever not?" asked Clara in astonishment. "I thought you two were such great friends."

"Don't you believe it," retorted the Knight. "He's been trying to do some of my work in Somaliland. I'm bound to admit," he added grudgingly, "that he's made almost as big a mess of it as I could myself, but that's neither here nor there."

Apparently the Knight wasn't either, for before Clara could even say good-bye, he had vanished head downwards into the earth of a badger. And the last Clara heard of him was a voice, which seemed to come from under a heap of wet blankets, and which said, "Draw me, indeed? Not they! All the R.A.s together couldn't do it."

Chapter VII

Playing with Fire

The Lizard took Clara to the cliff where they had seen the last of the Red Queen's ship. "It's there, your Majesty," it said in an awestruck voice. "It's there—waiting for you."

"What's there?" asked Clara, rather annoyed at being continually ordered about from one place to another.

"Why, the Unicorn, of course," said the Lizard. "It's come all the way to Blunderland to see you, and you mustn't keep it waiting."

Clara had forgotten all about the Unicorn, but she thought it might be nice to be able to say she had talked with a fabulous monster. So she went with the Lizard. She thought she saw the Constituent standing looking very sadly at her, but his outline was so dim that she was not quite sure.

"I hope he's not a Boojum," said Clara to herself, "for he seems a good sort of person, though rather common; and I don't want him to vanish away altogether."

"You'll make me one if you're not careful," said the Constituent, in a voice that seemed quite far off.

> "I've tried
> to help you
> as much as
> I could,
> but if
> you're
> going to
> have any-
> thing
> to say
> to the
> Lizard's
> foreign
> friends
> I shall
> certainly
> vanish
> away.
> And
> you'll
> never
> see me
> again.
> And
> then
> you'll
> cry."

Clara was not listening to him, however, for, standing right in front of her, was an enormous Unicorn, who seemed so big and overpowering that she gave a little scream.

"Hoch!" said the Unicorn in a very guttural voice.

"No, thank you, sir," said Clara very politely. "I'm only allowed wine at parties."

"How you voz?" said the Unicorn to Clara, in excellent English.

But Clara was still all eyes and no ears. She was gazing at the creature's lovely clothes. It was dressed in something which was neither a British admiral's uniform nor that of a Patagonian Gold-Stick-in-Waiting. "But for gorgeousness," said Clara afterwards, "the Unicorn might have been the Lord Mayor's coachman."

On the top of his helmet was a large sauerkraut in beautiful condition, and dangling from the end of his horn was a piece of the very largest sausage that Clara had ever seen.

"How you voz?" repeated the Unicorn in a louder voice. "Vos you stone broke in ze ear?"

"I beg your pardon, Sir, I don't understand German," said Clara very politely.

"So–o–o!" retorted the Unicorn, "that is for me very goot, for if you nodings know zen so much more easy it shall was for me mit you ze game of bluff to blay."

Clara thought this language rather vulgar, and did not quite understand it. "But then you see," she said to herself, "it's only a foreigner after all, and so I suppose we must make allowances for it."

"What game's that?" asked Clara, hoping that it was not one that involved any exertion.

"No," said the Unicorn, answering her thoughts. "It is ze 'Puss in ze Corner'. You ze Puss shall be, while I vos put you in ze corner."

"I know 'Puss in the Corner', of course," said Clara, for you see, she was a very intelligent child, and could almost always tell what people meant if it was explained to her first.

The Unicorn seemed delighted with the idea. It patted her head and said, "Goot schild, goot schild, you shall haf so nice a game mit me as you never saw;" and it pulled out of one of its boots a large map, which Clara at once recognized as representing the Western Hemisphere.

It also produced a very small chestnut, and some Germanic matches which struck only on the Pan. Then they lighted a fire, and the Unicorn blew and blew till there was quite a blaze, and such a crackle and splutter!

After that the Unicorn dropped the little chestnut into the middle of the fire and told Clara to pull it out.

"But I'm sure I should burn my fingers," said poor Clara.

"Zat," murmured the Unicorn gently, "zat is ze game. You shall pull all my chestnuts out of ze fire if you vas a goot girl, and zen you haf ze satisfagtion to see me eat. It is zan ze Zoo feeding time mosh more amusing, and I charge you very leedle for ze great exhibition."

"I do wish all the animals wouldn't order one about so," thought Clara to herself; but she was so frightened of the creature's great horn, which it said had been growing ever since 1870, that she did not like to refuse. And so she tried to pull the chestnut out.

"I don't call this 'Puss in the Corner'," said Clara.

"He voz not *called* 'Puss in ze Corner', said the Unicorn. "I said he voz *like* 'Puss in ze Corner'. He is *called* 'Venezuela'."

"Oh! That's its name, is it?" asked Clara.

"No, it voz not his *name*. His name voz 'Bluff'," explained the Unicorn.

"'Bluff'? I never heard of such a game before. Well, I'm glad I know what it is at last," said Clara, who was getting quite muddled.

"Zat's only his *name*," said the Unicorn. "If you vant to know what zat game really *is*, he *is* 'Heads I shall vin, tails you shall lose'."

Clara thought it was no use trying to talk to her strange companion, so she set herself again to try and pull the chestnut out of the fire, but it was so hot that she wished she had never begun to play this game at all.

She noticed, however, that as soon as she began the Unicorn got very fidgety, and kept looking up into the sky as though it expected something to fall upon them.

"What is the matter?" she asked.

"Oh, nodings," said the Unicorn. "I only vonders how ze Monrostrous Crow shall like it. You see, dis place is to his nest very close, and he voz a bird of ze kvick temper. But go on, leedle girl, I brodtecd you."

Then it became dark, and the air seemed filled with the most tremendous flapping of great wings, which made so much wind that it blew out the Unicorn's fire.

IT WAS THE MONROSTROUS CROW.

"Git!" screamed the Crow to the Unicorn as soon as it could get its breath (it had only just finished a fight with the

Tammany Tiger, and was consequently a little flurried). "You've no call to be getting this young lady into mischief, and you know it. I'll have none of this disgraceful roasting on my place. And as for you, my dear," turning to Clara as it spoke, "whatever made you take up with that Fabulous Monster?"

"Shoost drow one shtone to him," whispered the Unicorn, "and I runs mine horn into him vhile he shall look ze ozzer vay."

But Clara saw that, for all its brave talk, the Unicorn was dreadfully frightened, and meant to run away the moment the Monrostrous Crow took its eye off it. Besides, she thought she liked the bird a good deal better than the beast. So she only said, "I'm sure, Mr Crow, I'm very sorry to have disturbed you, and I wo'n't do it again."

"Guess I don't expect *you* to know any better," said the Crow. "And," it continued angrily, "I'll make that darned Unicorn see stars and stripes if it comes here again. But," it added, in a kinder tone, "you shouldn't play with strangers. Wait till the Red Queen comes back. There, there," it added, as Clara began to cry. "We sha'n't quarrel, but you'd better take that creature away. So long."

All this time the Unicorn had been shrinking and shrinking in size till it was only about as big as Clara, and was trying to hide behind her skirts.

"Kom avay, kom avay, leedle girl," she heard it say, "and I show you anoder game much more nicer as zat," and it hurried her off as quickly as ever it could.

"You voz not blay fair," complained the Unicorn, getting brave again as soon as they were out of sight of the Crow. "You voz not blay zat game ze English vay. You should of yourself altogeder overcome mit shame be."

"Why, what have I done now?" asked Clara, plaintively; but she thought to herself: "The Unicorn isn't half as big as it looked at first. I needn't be frightened of it, after all." Still the horn looked very sharp, and she thought it might be strong enough to give her a pin prick if she did not take care.

"Ach!" said the Unicorn. "Ven I say you not blay fair, I mean you do not blay ze game according to his rules and regulations. You sheat me."

"I'm sure I didn't," Clara answered, indignantly. "I never cheat. Sometimes," she added, as an afterthought, "perhaps I don't play quite according to the rules. But that's only in those muddly games like 'Taxes and Tariffs' and things. I'm sure nobody understands *them*."

"You sheat me," repeated the Unicorn, sulkily. "Ze rule of zat game vos zat you shall fight ze Monrostrous Crow. Zen, if he shall vin, I gets your leedle legacy, and if you vins, I makes mineself one nice coat out of ze fezzers from him. He is a most amusing game, and I haf blayed him before. If you come all ze vay mit me I show you lots of fezzers from ze Austrian Eagle I get shoost zat vay.... Zere is no one vot can blay zat game so better as me. But nefer mind! Ze Red Kveen she teach it you some days."

"I think I'd rather not play it with you any more if you don't mind, Sir," returned Clara, rather timidly. "I'm sure I should never be able to play it really well, and it wouldn't give a professional like yourself" (here the Unicorn smiled and looked pleased) "any satisfaction to beat an amateur like me, would it?"

"Dat is shoost vat it vould," said the Unicorn. "Somebodys vrom your country vill haf to blay him mit me somedays." And it added, half to itself, "I only hope it shall not be zat Red Kveen of yours. She blay him mit one long spoon, she do, and she blay to vin ven she blay. But now," it went on aloud, "ve blay ze ozzer game I tells you of. You gifs me all ze zings you in your far-too-much-befilled pockets haf, and I makes you one of all ze odder most favoured nations."

"But," said Clara doubtfully, "I've got a lot of Colonial produce in my pockets, and I think I'd rather keep it myself, if you've no objection."

"Nefer mind," returned the Unicorn. "I gif you lots of goot dings in egschange. I gifs you a peautiful leedle knife mit vich you your fingers cut cannot because he voz made in Shermany, and, oh! lots of dings almost as sheap as zey are nasty, and I does all your drading for you and safes you all ze drouble."

Suddenly the Unicorn became very pale and stood staring into space. Clara turned and saw the Red Queen rushing towards them at her usual furious pace.

In her hand she held a circular object which looked like a huge plum pudding.

Clara felt a little uneasy. She knew that somehow she had done wrong in playing with the Unicorn, and she was afraid the Red Queen would scold her.

"The worst of it is," said Clara to herself, "whatever I do seems to be wrong, and I'm sure I don't know why."

"No, my dear," said the Constituent, who had come back. "That's not the worst of it. If you only *did* know, why, then there might be some hope for you."

His voice was shrill now, and Clara thought he had become rather impertinent in his manner; but his outline was quite dim, and he was, as Clara said, "the ghost of his former self."

By this time the Red Queen was quite close to them, and the Unicorn looked as if it would like to run away, but as soon as its eyes lighted upon the rich pudding it stood still, licking its lips.

Ever since the Monrostrous Crow had been out of sight, the Unicorn had been growing larger and larger, but as the Red Queen approached it began to shrink again.

The Red Queen was too triumphant and happy to scold Clara, although she looked very coldly at the Unicorn.

"Mein gootness! Vot a peautiful bouddings!" exclaimed the Unicorn.

"It *is* beautiful," said Clara, clapping her hands.

"Yes," said the Red Queen proudly. "It is the finest ever boiled. It is the Commercial World, and I hold it in the hollow of my hand."

"So you voz," said the Unicorn, quite politely. "But voz he not rahzer heavy? Shall I hold him for you one leedle minute?"

"You must ask the Lion first," said the Red Queen. "It's *his* pudding."

"He voz always asleep," said the Unicorn. "I shall only on ze head of him sit mineself, and zen I eat it all."

The Red Queen merely tossed her head. "Now, Clara," she said, "you're the proper person to take charge of the pudding, though I got it. Take it, and mind you don't let it drop. I'll keep an eye on the Unicorn and see that he doesn't snatch it from you until you get to the Lion. And then just let them fight for it."

Chapter VIII

Pudding and Pugilists

However, while they were speaking the Lion and the White King appeared arm in arm, and the Unicorn immediately joined them. The White King seemed to be telling the Lion funny stories and trying to make the great beast smile. But Clara noticed that, though the Lion pretended to be amused at them, he was yawning very much and looked like falling asleep. She thought she heard him mutter once or twice to himself, "Never do, never do. Most unpractical." Still the White King kept on talking, just as though he were a phonograph which had been wound up and couldn't stop, and the Unicorn seemed rather to approve of him than otherwise. The Lion was evidently

very old, and seemed very, very weary, though every now and then he shot a glance from his half-closed eyes, that made Clara wonder whether he was quite as drowsy as he looked.

"Shoost you see zis great pig boudding I haf vound," said the Unicorn, pushing Clara forward with the dish in her hand. "I voz so kind I comes to share it mit you. You shall have ze dough, ze dish, and Clara. I voz only eat ze plums mineselfs."

"Thankee," said the Lion, in tones which sounded as though a blanket were over his head. "You're very good, I'm sure, but there's nothing the matter with my digestion so far. I can eat it all."

"Vot? You no gifs me ze plums? Zen for ze bouddings we shall fight," said the Unicorn, half to itself.

The Lion seemed to guess the meaning of the Unicorn's muttered words, for he stiffened all over and became effusively and offensively polite.

"Did I understand you to say something about Canadian tariffs?" he gently remarked. And the Lion chuckled sleepily as he spoke.

All this time the White King was standing first on one leg and then on the other—which seemed to be his favourite amusement—and kept making unsuccessful attempts to tell another story, which began with the words, "Once upon a time there was a Tabernacle."

Neither the Lion nor the Unicorn paid the least attention to him, and Clara felt quite sorry at the number of times they interrupted him.

"Besides," she said to herself, "I *should* like to know how that story ended."

"It hasn't got any end," remarked the Lion, slowly, as though he had read her thoughts. "He's been trying to tell it for years, and nobody has ever been able to see the point of it yet. The White Queen says she knows it too. But she's always so confused that I ca'n't make head or tail of what she means.

Besides, they both tell it quite differently. You'd hardly believe it, my dear," he went on, "but sometimes both of them try and tell it together, and then my poor head gets so muddled I ca'n't remember anything at all."

"You're very rude," said the White King, wiping the tears from his eyes. "If you go on saying things like that I shall go right away and play all by myself on the turf. So there!"

"Ze reason," addressing the Lion, "zat you voz not gombrehend," suddenly interjected the Unicorn, who had been very impatient at all this talk for some time. "Ze reason voz blain. You voz decadent."

"Am I?" said the Lion, in a tone of indifference. "Any way it's better than being bumptious."

"Ach!" neighed the Unicorn. "You can no longer fight. Once you voz anytings. Now you voz nobodys. I schnap mine hoofs to you." And, to Clara's great alarm, the Unicorn began running round and round the Lion and kicking unwholesome little bits off the big pudding which she had placed on the ground between them.

Clara was so frightened that she got behind a tree. In the meantime the behaviour of the Unicorn got worse and worse, and she said to herself, "I know that horrid Unicorn will get all the pudding, and the poor dear, sleepy old Lion wo'n't get any at all, and, oh dear, I don't know what I ought to do."

Curiously enough, the Lion seemed to take it all quite as a matter of course. He had very slowly and deliberately put on a pair of boxing-gloves, "in order," as he explained, "not to hurt the Unicorn if it came to a fight after all." When he had done this he remarked, "Gr-r-r-h, gr-r-r-r-uulph," once or twice, lay down, folded his paws, and immediately went fast asleep on top of the pudding.

"There!" exclaimed the White King. "That's what he always does now, and who's to wake him up, I'm sure I don't know. I've tried everything—opium, soothing syrup, and even throwing dust in his eyes. You know, there's nothing like dust for keeping one awake."

"I should have thought throwing water in his face or shouting in his ears would have been better," said Clara, doubtfully.

"I didn't say there was nothing better than dust," retorted the White King rather angrily. "I said there was nothing *like* it"; and Clara felt that this was only too true.

All this time the Unicorn was running round and round the Lion, shouting, "Trade! Trade! Beautiful Trade!" at the very top of its voice. ("It made a most dreadful noise," Clara said afterwards, "and never stopped for an instant.")

The Lion's snores only got gruffer and gruffer, and Clara was beginning to think she would really have to go away and leave him to be eaten up by the Unicorn when she saw the Red Queen come running towards them.

"Here she is at last!" said the delighted child. "Now I'm sure we shall get something done!"

"I don't hold with *her*," said the White King, pointing with his thumb to the Queen over his shoulder. "She's never been what I call sympathetic," and he strolled a little way with a queer expression of offended dignity, which made Clara very much inclined to laugh.

"Good riddance of bad rubbish, I say," exclaimed the Red Queen, pettishly, when she came up. "I'd take his head off for ninepence, if I had my way. But what's all this?" she went on. "Here's that Unicorn at it again, and you've been and let the Lion go to sleep, you silly child!"

"If you please, ma'am," said Clara very humbly, "I didn't know what to do, and I was afraid the Lion might eat me if I tried to wake him up."

"I don't know about *you*," retorted the Queen, "but he wo'n't eat me. I can manage him." And as she spoke she seized hold of the Lion's tail and twisted it until Clara thought it would come off in her hands.

After a long time the Lion gradually opened first one eye and then the other, gave a tremendous yawn, and said, "Ah! Unicorn! You here still? Don't you find all that exercise very fatiguing? I wish you'd let me sleep in peace."

"The Unicorn's stealing the pudding!" shouted the Queen as soon as she saw he was awake. "Get up and protect yourself."

"All right," said the Lion, rubbing his eyes. "Oh dear, how very sleepy I do feel, to be sure."

But just as he was in the middle of another yawn the Queen gave his tail an extra twist which seemed to wake him up completely. He stood up with a loud roar, at which the Unicorn instantly turned and fled with its tail between its legs. Underneath the Lion was a broken dish,

BUT NO PUDDING.

At first Clara thought that the Unicorn had stolen it, but when she saw how enormously fat the Lion had grown in that short time she guessed where the pudding had gone.

"Why, I do declare," said Clara in amazement, "if the Lion hasn't been and eaten the pudding in his sleep."

"That's the way he does most things, my dear," replied the Red Queen. "It's a habit he's got."

Chapter IX

Hatched Out

"Come here, my dear," said the White King, who had come back as soon as he saw that the Red Queen had left Clara and was patting the Lion approvingly on the back. "Come for a walk with me. I think we might be friends."

"I hope so, I'm sure," said Clara.

"You see," said the White King, "my plan is always partially to ingratiate myself with people, and then to—"

"And then to, what?" asked Clara.

"And then to go off and impartially ingratiate myself with some one else, of course," said the White King.

"Well," said Clara, as the King turned off in another direction, "this is a curious walk. You don't seem to know which way you're going."

"There's no fun in a walk if you only go in one direction, or if you know where you're going to," said the White King.

"I'm afraid," said Clara, "we shall soon have to go different ways."

"Don't be too sure of that," said the King. "When you get into Opposition-street—which, if you go on losing your way you'll soon do—you'll find me there. In fact," he added, "I live there now. Cool, shady, and not at all an unpleasant situation, when you get used to it."

Suddenly the King turned to Clara, and said, "Here we are at last."

"Dear me," thought Clara. "How he changes the conversation! He's as bad as Mr F.'s Aunt, in that book that I couldn't get through because it was so vulgar."

But the King was getting excited. "Now, my child," he said, "I'm going to show you something worth seeing. There's going to be a Grand Review of my splendid Army."

They were in a large field, which Clara thought looked very barren. In the middle of it three men and a boy were pitching a torn and tattered looking tent. Then they unfurled a beautiful banner with some long words on it which Clara tried to spell out, but she couldn't understand them at all. They planted the banner very carefully in front of the tent.

"That's the Tabernacle you heard me telling that foolish old Lion about," said the King proudly, "and they've gone inside to put their uniforms on."

When the men and the boy came out of the tent they were dressed in the brilliant uniform of the Tabernaculars.

She liked the boy best, for he made such a dear little drummer, and stood by the banner beating as hard as he could. The men stood up stiffly and saluted the King, who nodded encouragingly to them. Then they began to march with great dignity and very slowly. It seemed, however, that they only marched round the tent, for before the last soldier had disappeared behind it, the first one had appeared again; and so they kept on, going round and round, until Clara felt quite giddy.

"Ah!" said the King proudly. "I see you're admiring my Army. Every one of that vast host you see defiling over there is an out-and-out Half-a-Leaguer, and would cheerfully lay down his life for the great principle I represent—if only," he went on rather sadly, "I could remember what it was."

"But they aren't a vast host at all," Clara replied. "I've counted them up ever so many times, and there are only three besides the drummer."

"You don't understand these things at all," the King retorted very angrily. "Thats the way an Army is *always* represented on the stage. If you want to do anything nowadays you must be theatrical. Some people are *never* satisfied."

"Still," Clara persisted, "it isn't quite like a real Army, you know."

"Do you think I don't know that?" said the poor King. "But it's the best I can do."

Clara was just going to say how sorry she felt for him, when the King exclaimed, "I've got something else to show you. Come and see my Informers. You've no idea what useful creatures they are. I keep two of them—one to tell me what has happened, and one to tell me what hasn't. But," he went on, "I don't know how it is; they seem to get their duties mixed up every now and then."

"That must be rather awkward, isn't it?" asked Clara.

"You may say that, my dear," returned the King. "But come and look at them."

"Where are they?" asked Clara, who was getting rather tired. "Shall we have to go far?"

"They are always on the spot, of course," said the King, "or, at least, they say so."

Then, just down the road, Clara saw two very funny looking creatures, who were throwing themselves into the most peculiar attitudes. First of all they seemed to be abusing one another, and then one kissed his hand, while the other made friendly signs to him. All at once they caught sight of the King, and before Clara could count two they were both pouring out information as hard as ever they could. And most extraordinary information it was.

"The King may say what he likes," thought Clara, "but, to *my* mind, both of them are telling stories. I don't believe a word of all that stuff about Sea Serpents, and Big

Gooseberries, and about the Decline of England, and the White King being the greatest man that ever lived.

"But," she went on aloud, "would you please tell me why your Informers make those curious movements?"

"The attitudes of this one—" replied the King, pointing to one who looked like a hare, and who handed him a number of newspaper cuttings as he spoke, "—the attitudes of this one are Anglo-Saxon. Now those of the other—" indicating a very disreputable-looking creature in a swallowtail coat, "—are Russo-German."

"Thank you," replied Clara. "Now I understand for the first time what they mean by the attitude of the Press."

"Not you," retorted the King. "That's a thing you'll never understand. But they *are* beauties, aren't they?" he went on. "I prefer the Russo-German one myself. He's the more trustworthy of the two. You see the other *does* tell the truth *sometimes*, which is very confusing; but this one *never* does, and that makes it so simple."

Just then Clara was startled by a piercing shriek, and, turning, saw the White Queen limping heavily towards the wood as hard as ever she could go. She was shouting at the top of her voice, "Help! HELP! My shadow's after me," but the White King made no attempt to go to her rescue.

"There's the White Queen," said Clara, "and I'm sure she's being pursued."

"Very likely," remarked the King, without even looking up.

"But aren't you going to help her?" asked Clara, indignantly. "I'm sure she's being chased by an enemy."

"It'll be some Imperialist or other," the King remarked slowly. "This part of the country's full of 'em. They turn up in all sorts of unlikely places."

Clara was so disgusted with the King's callousness that she determined to go to the Queen's help herself. So she ran after her and soon caught her up.

"Thank you, my dear," the Queen said, as Clara gently helped her to a seat. "I'm sure I don't know what I should do if it were not for you. You help me a great deal oftener than you think. Just then my passive resistance was almost overcome."

"I don't know what you call passive," said Clara. "You were making noise enough I'm sure; but," she went on suddenly, recognizing a curious likeness to Crumpty-Bumpty, "surely, when I saw you last, you were in the shell, so to speak?"

"An egg, my dear," returned the Queen. "A nice, round, smooth egg. That's what I was. But those happy days are over. So many people sat upon me that at last I was hatched. And this," she said, in a melancholy tone, "is what I have come to."

"Well," said Clara, rather doubtfully, unable to think of anything else to comfort her, "it's rather grand to be a Queen. At least I suppose so."

"Much good there is in that," retorted the Queen, pettishly. "How would you like it if you were married to the White King, and couldn't get rid of him anyhow?"

"I shouldn't like it at all," replied Clara, who was a very truthful child. "I should think he was rather a trial."

"Rather a trial!" almost screamed the Queen. "He's worse than a verdict." And she began to cry.

"Oh, please don't do that," begged the little girl. "Let me tidy you up a bit, and then you'll feel ever so much better. Why, what a state you're in!" she went on. And certainly the poor Queen looked as if she was almost falling to pieces. "Let me comb your hair for you, and brush off some of this mud. Why, you must have been rolling in it."

"It isn't my fault if I have," grumbled the Queen. "I've been dragged through it. But you'll always go on helping me, wo'n't you? You're the best friend I ever had, if you only knew it."

This last sentence puzzled Clara a great deal.

Chapter X

Under the Peer Tree

When Clara had pinned her up as best she could, the White Queen, who had caught sight of her Russo-German Informer, hurried off to meet him, without so much as a "thank you". All she said was, "Isn't he a dear creature? I'm sure he'll tell me some scandal I can spread about."

Clara was too disgusted to follow her, and strolled into the wood out of which the Queen had come so hurriedly.

Suddenly she was startled by a noise which sounded like something between a groan and a sneeze, with a sort of whistling shriek in it. She was rather afraid it might be caused by some savage animal, like an Irish Representative; but when she saw the Red Queen in the distance coming towards her she determined to show her how courageous she really was, and slowly walked towards the place from which the sound seemed to come, only hoping that the Queen would overtake her before she reached it.

When she had gone a little way into the wood she caught sight of what seemed to be the top of a night-cap sticking out from behind a tree. The tassel was shaking and quivering with the dreadful sounds, and she felt sure that the night-cap belonged to the person who was making them.

"Come," she said to herself. "Whatever it is, it ca'n't be anything very terrible if it's wearing a night-cap, for that old Drummond Wolf in 'Red Riding Hood' was only a fairy-tale creature, and couldn't be true." So she determined to find out what it was.

When she had got far enough she found that it was the fg who was lying under a peer-tree fast asleep, and snoring like an angry steam-engine.

"Dear me!" said Clara to the Red Queen, who had come up by this time. "Why, I'd quite forgotten his existence."

"Had you?" remarked the Queen, rather crossly. "I hadn't. It's lucky for you he goes on dreaming in that peaceful way."

"What does he dream about?" asked Clara, who was always very curious about anything to do with psychical research.

"You, mostly, child," answered the Queen. "In fact you're really only a part of his dream. You don't suppose you're real, do you?"

"Of course I am," said Clara indignantly. "I wo'n't be teased with philosophic doubts of *that* kind, at any rate."

"You wo'n't make yourself a bit realler by writing books about it, you know," remarked the Queen. "Why, whether you believe it or not, if that King was to wake—really to wake, I mean—you'd go squash, just like a roseberry. But," she went on in a kinder tone, "you needn't be afraid. I've been married to him for years and years, and I've never known him to wake up yet. Even when he seems to be awake he's really only talking in his sleep."

"Dooon't he ever dream about *you*?" asked Clara, rather hastily, for she didn't at all like the turn the conversation was taking.

"Now and then," answered the Queen. "I'm his nightmare. He got into that state," the Queen went on, "through smoking strong Cavendish under this peer-tree, and I don't think he'll ever wake up again. I'm sure," she said wearily, "I've tried all *I* know to rouse him."

"Perhaps it's more healthy for him to be as he is," said Clara. "I wouldn't try to wake him up if I were you. Isn't there a proverb about 'letting sleeping dukes lie', or something of that kind? He might be dangerous if he woke up altogether."

"Rubbish!" retorted the Queen angrily. "He'd *never* come awake enough to do anything serious. You don't suppose I should ever have let him be King if there was any risk of that kind, do you?"

"Look here," she went on, and then she began to walk round and round him, and, as Clara described it, "to hypocrize him with cannibalistic signs." Every now and then she shouted in his ear some mysterious word which sounded like "Protection", or something of that kind; but the King only muttered in his sleep, "Ah, yes, yes. Property, property, pro—" and turned over on the other side.

There was a bladder full of peas lying beside him, apparently for the purpose of enabling his friends to rouse him; but though the Queen took it from him and rattled it on his head as hard as ever she could, it produced not the slightest effect.

"Ca'n't you talk, you lazy thing?" shouted the Queen. "Here's this young lady come to give you her views on preferential tariffs, and you lie there like a Royal Commission all the time."

"Indeed I've not," said Clara indignantly. "I shouldn't think of such a thing. You oughtn't to say such a thing when you know perfectly well that I've no settled convictions."

"*He* has, though," replied the Queen. "You wait a bit and you'll see. Watch the effect of this," and she suddenly shouted, "Taxes on food—taxes on food!" till Clara was quite shocked.

The effect on the King was extraordinary. His eyes remained closed, but he instantly sat bolt upright, "just," as Clara thought, "as if he were really wide awake," and said in a monotonous voice, "Eh, what—what? Taxes on food! Not if I know it. You'll have the whole of Blunderland in an uproar if you go talking like that."

"Well, I should like to know who's going to stop ME if I choose to," retorted the Queen with an acid smile. "*You* wo'n't, anyhow."

"It'll come to a separation, I suppose," said the King mechanically. "I've thought it would for a long time. You're too fast, far, far too fast, and I hate being hurried. We shall have to part. If we don't, I shall really be woke up one of these days. It's worse than being married to a Bandersnatch."

"How dreadful!" said Clara, who hated to think of such a thing. "Couldn't there be an investigation, or an inquiry, or something, into the differences between you two first?" She was really anxious to make peace between them, because, in the first place, she was afraid of the talk which a separation would cause, and, in the second, because she could not quite make up her mind whose side she ought to take.

"Of course, *I* don't mind inquiries," said the King gloomily. "But it wo'n't be of the least use. She—" yawning at the Red Queen as he spoke "—she's made up her mind long ago, and she's that obstinate," he went on, forgetting his grammar in his indignation, "as never was. Once she's said a thing she sticks to it right or wrong. Not like you, my dear—you're a good, obedient child; and anybody, I'm sure, could persuade you to give up anything that wasn't approved of, couldn't they?"

"I hope so, sir," said Clara, blushing at this well-merited praise. "I've given up nearly everything I really care about, even Hughie and the licensed Victualler."

"Well, give up the Red Queen," said the King, still talking in his sleep. "It'll be better for you than anything you ever gave up before. She'll never let you have a wink of sleep, and, after all, sleep is the great what's-his-name, you know."

"You just try and give me up," said the Queen, spitefully, "and I'll have you black-balled!"

"Oh, dear! Oh, dear!" said Clara, beginning to cry. "What *shall* I do?"

"Do?" growled the King. "Why, do as I do. Strike out a line for yourself. Mine's sleep, and a very good line, too. You might try ghosts, or philosophy, or anything of that kind."

"She's no good at those things," said the Queen, with great decision. "Crotchet-work would be better."

"Well, anyway leave *me* alone," mumbled the King. "If you two go on like this I shall really wake up altogether one of these days, and then I don't know *what* would happen!" and he began to snore again.

"Give me your hand, child," said the Queen, "and come away. There's nothing to be done with *him*."

But Clara had been so much impressed with what the King had said about striking out a line for herself, that she replied with great dignity, "Thank you, I'd rather not! I'm going to be independent for the future!"

"Please yourself," replied the Queen with a short laugh. "It wo'n't last long."

"You're both rather cross," said Clara, looking back at the King as they walked away. "Do you think you *will* have to separate?"

"No," replied the Queen, confidently. "He's more sensible than he looks. He'll dream about what I said and come round some day. When he finds out that the household expenses don't go up after all, we shall be friends again."

"I'm so glad you think so," said Clara. "I mustn't let you lead me about. But still I hope you'll be happy."

"I expect we shall have. to part for a time," remarked the Queen, thoughtfully. "There'd have been no danger of it if only you'd backed me up properly. But there! You're such a timid child, I suppose one couldn't expect it!"

CHAPTER XI

A Tight Place

"Well," said the Red Queen, after they had gone on like this for some little way, "if you wo'n't take my hand I shall be off. I've got lots and lots of other things to attend to. Indeed," she went on pensively, "I have to attend to most things. I'm sure I don't know how they'll manage when I retire. A pretty mess everything'll get into then!"

She turned away as she spoke, and Clara, who felt most dreadfully naughty and wilful, never even looked round to see which way she had taken, but walked on by herself with her head in the air.

"I *will* show them that I am a *real* Queen," she said to herself.

She had not gone far when she came on a quaint-looking house.

"Why, it must be an inn!" she exclaimed, and hurried along as fast as she could to see what it was like.

She was quite hungry by this time, and was thinking how exciting it would be to go in all by herself and order her own tea. She had never done such a thing before, for her Aunt had never let her go anywhere without a respectable nursemaid. But Clara was feeling very independent just then as she went up to the door. Her courage received a little shock, however, when she looked up and saw a terrifying signboard which creaked dismally as the wind blew it to and fro.

She read the landlord's name.

"I wonder what sort of a person he is," she said aloud. "I expect he's some jolly round dear old thing just like Crumpty-Bumpty or some one."

"He's not. He's the Black Knight, and he's an ogre. I wouldn't go in there if I were you," said a little voice at her elbow. Clara looked round and saw that it was the Constituent, who had somehow managed to follow her.

"I wish you wouldn't keep bobbing up like that," said Clara, very crossly. "Ca'n't you make up your mind either to go or to stay? You're so upsetting."

"I shall keep bobbing up, as you call it," replied the Constituent, "for months and months, and if you're upset it will be all your own fault."

Clara thought that the Constituent got more and more rude every time he spoke to her, and she knew that what he said about the innkeeper being an ogre must be all stories, because ogres are only in fairy tales, which she hadn't believed in since she was *quite* a little girl, except, of course, those that the Unicorn told her.

His words, however, made her wonder what the innkeeper could be like. So she asked him why he had called him an ogre.

"Because he says words which you wouldn't understand, like 'Fe! Fo! Fum!'" said the Constituent.

"Fe! *Fi*! Fo! Fum! you mean," corrected Clara, who was very particular as far as the classics were concerned. "Fe! *Fi*! Fo! Fum!"

"No, I don't," said the Constituent, sulkily. "*He* doesn't say 'Fie!' It's the people that hear him who say that."

"Well," said. Clara, "anyway, saying things doesn't make a person an ogre. It's eating—"

"Well then," interrupted the Constituent, "he's a fire-eater, and you'd better not go in."

"I see what you mean," said Clara rather scornfully. "You mean he's a sort of conjurer, not an ogre."

"He used to juggle with figures, certainly," admitted the Constituent, "and remarkably well too."

"Then I shall certainly go in and see him," cried Clara joyfully, for of all things, next of course to sitting up all night, she loved being mystified.

The door opened and the Black Knight came out. He looked rather fierce, Clara thought, but his manners were nice.

He at once walked up to Clara and shook her hand with great warmth.

"I'm so glad to see you again, you dear old thing," he said. "Why, we haven't met since that party of your Aunt Sarum's. I've taken this inn now," he went on. "It's a little draughty, perhaps, and there are not so many customers as I could wish, but on the whole I like it better than the old place. In fact," he continued, "I'm resigned to it."

Clara couldn't think what he was talking about, for she didn't remember ever to have met him before. He seemed very nice and kind, however, and his language was ornamented with the most beautiful flowers of expression. They reminded her so much of what the cat said when the parrot caught hold of its tail, that she didn't like to say she really hadn't the pleasure of his acquaintance.

"I presume," she said, politely, "I have the honour of addressing the Black Knight?"

"You have," replied the innkeeper, "and I'm very glad to see you appreciate how great it is."

Clara thought that was a question of taste, but she only said: "I wonder why you don't wear your beautiful armour. I'm sure if I had a suit like yours I should never take it off."

"Ah, but then, you see, I don't want *any* Protection, and you do," retorted the Knight.

"Do I?" asked Clara. "I don't really know, but it *sounds* nice."

"Wo'n't you walk into my parlour?" said the Black Knight, pointing to his house.

"Don't go in," whispered the Constituent, but so faintly that Clara scarcely heard him. "That is just what the Spider said, and you know how that ended."

Clara took no notice of the warning, but told the Knight that she would be delighted to go indoors with him, and they moved off together, the poor little Constituent still following behind and trying to whisper warnings in Clara's ear.

When they got into the hall the first thing Clara noticed was a twopenny cheque lying on the floor. Clara thought the Knight must have dropped it by accident, and so she picked it up in order to give it to him.

She found that it was marked: "N.S. Refer to drawer". She thought these letters must have some meaning, though she could not imagine what it was, and when she handed the cheque to the Knight she ventured to ask him.

To her surprise, he immediately got very red in the face, and seemed quite confused.

"They mean nothing, *nothing* at all," he said, after a long pause. "I give you my word—and that's as good as an Exchequer Bond—that there's *no* meaning in them."

He was so emphatic in his manner and seemed so much annoyed that Clara was afraid she must have said something very rude, and she gently remarked: "I'm so sorry if I've hurt your feelings. Don't let's talk about the nasty cheque any more."

"I'm sure *I* don't want to," replied the Knight. "It's rather a sore subject with me just now."

Clara tried to think of some way of turning the conversation, but for some time she couldn't think of anything to say, and they stood looking at one another in gloomy silence.

"Wouldn't you like to be independent of them all, and do just what you like, and never have anybody to scold you, or interfere with you?" asked the Knight at last.

"I should, indeed," answered Clara. "That's just what I've always wanted."

"Now," said the Knight, in an insinuating tone, "if that's what you really want, I think I can help you. You see this key?"

"Yes," replied Clara, who noticed that he held one in his hand.

"Well," said the Knight, "they call this the Key of the Situation, and I very rarely let it out of my hands."

"Don't you, really?" asked Clara, thinking it was a very small key to have such a long name.

"It unlocks the door," said the Knight, "of a beautiful little room which I particularly want to show you, where you can do exactly as you like," and he pointed to a little door in the wall, which was half concealed by a curtain.

"If you let him take you in there," said the tiny voice of the Constituent, who still kept behind her, "you'll never get out again. You'll always be his prisoner."

"Nonsense!" said Clara, over her shoulder, and giving a little toss of her head as she spoke. "Nonsense!"

"If you wo'n't be warned, there's no use in my staying here any longer," said the poor little creature, with a sob in its voice; and Clara saw him hurrying out of the hall.

"Did you hear what he said?" Clara asked the Black Knight when the Constituent had disappeared. "I believe I must have offended him."

"Oh, that's nothing! I am always doing that," said the Knight. "I never take any notice of him, and you'd better not either. But now I'll show you over the house."

As he spoke he handed her the key, and she pulled the curtain aside and unlocked the little door.

Clara found that it led into a little room, which seemed so tiny that she said to the Knight, "I don't believe I can get into it after all."

The fact was that from the moment she took the key in her hand she began to grow in importance so much that she was already almost twice as big as she was when she entered the inn.

"Oh, yes, you can," replied the Knight. "You only want to stoop a little." And when Clara bent her head she found she could just manage to squeeze in.

No sooner had she done so, than the Knight shut the door with a bang, and began to shout, "I've caught her! I've caught her! Hooray! Hooray!"

"Let me out at once," cried Clara, who was dreadfully frightened, and who felt she was still growing.

"Never," said the Knight through the keyhole. "I'm not going to let you out at all. I'm going to smother you."

"Help!" cried Clara. "Oh, wo'n't somebody help me out of this? I'll be good, indeed I will."

"Too late, too late," wailed the voice of the Constituent under the window. "The Black Knight's got you and he'll keep you now. Why didn't you listen to me?"

A Tight Place

Clara was so ashamed at the way in which she had allowed herself to be trapped that she felt cross with everybody. She could just get her hand out of the window and she made a grab at the place where she thought the Constituent was.

"For," she said to herself, "if I could only catch him perhaps the Black Knight would take him in exchange for me."

She didn't manage to get hold of him however, but she heard a little shriek, and there was a sound of broken glass, just as if somebody had fallen into one of the looking-glass houses Clara had been told not to throw stones at.

"Oh, dear! Oh, dear!" she sobbed. "Whatever *will* become of me?"

"I shall smother you with statistics," said the voice of the Black Knight, who had apparently climbed on to the roof and was shouting down the chimney. Clara didn't in the least know what "statistics" were, but it sounded as if they were something very dreadful, and she began to scream louder than ever.

Presently bushels of statistics began to pour down the chimney. They were very like tin-tacks in appearance, but they seemed to be poisoned, for they gave her the most excruciating pain wherever they touched her.

The Knight had evidently any amount of them at his disposal, for they came down the chimney by thousands, and poor Clara made up her mind that she was done for altogether.

Just when she had given up all hope, she heard the voice of the Red Queen calling outside, "Clara! Clara! Where *has* that silly child got to?"

"I'm locked in here!" screamed Clara. "The Black Knight's smothering me with statistics with sharp points! Help! Help!"

"I'll statistic him!" shouted the Queen. "Only let me get at him!"

But this was just what the Knight evidently intended her not to do, for by the sounds above her she guessed he was trying to hide himself in the chimney.

"I saw him!" said the Queen. "He's in the chimney now. Kick, Clara! Kick! Kick as hard as ever you can!"

Clara could get her foot a little way up the chimney and as she realized at last that her only hope was to follow the

A Tight Place

Queen's directions, she drew it back and kicked as hard as she could.

"There he goes!" shouted the Queen. "Catch him, somebody! Don't let him fall on the other side of the hedge!"

("But," as the Queen told her afterwards, "he never was caught. When you kicked him out he exploded in a loud Report, which was subsequently issued by the Cobden Club, and, of course, nobody ever heard of him again.")

"You've been a bad child!" said the Queen, putting her head in at the window and speaking very angrily. "You've been warned by me, and warned by the Constituent whom you treated so badly, and it's all been no good! You'll come to a bad end, you see if you don't!"

"I'll never, never, do it again!" sobbed Clara; but the Queen went on scolding her just the same.

The scolding was so severe that it made Clara feel small enough to get out of the window, tiny as it was.

At first she ran off into the wood, but presently she sidled timidly up to the Queen, who said sharply, "I hope it'll be a lesson to you!" when Clara came up to her.

"It will, indeed!" replied the child, very humbly. "I'll never despise a warning again. And, oh! Please your Majesty, I've picked this orchid for you, and I've come to say 'Ditto' to you, and I'll never say anything but 'Ditto' again!"

"That's a good little girl!" said the Queen, in a kinder tone. "And now, since you're going to be good, you shall come with me to the great picnic."

"That *will* be nice!" said Clara, delighted if to find the Queen had forgiven her.

"That depends," said the Queen.

Chapter XII

The Picnic

"I must impress upon you," said the Red Queen, as Clara trotted obediently by her side, "the necessity of being upon your very best behaviour at the picnic to which I am taking you. You'll find a great many people there of whom you know little or nothing, and some, considering that you never read the newspapers, of whom you have never even heard. Take care you are very nice to them."

Clara promised to behave as well as she could, but privately she thought her manners were a great deal better than the Red Queen's. "There's a Brummagem something about her tone after all," she said to herself. For you see Clara, had been accustomed to go into the most *exclusive* Society, and very properly regarded everybody who didn't belong to her own family as of no importance whatever.

However, she had learned by this time that there are some things you had better not *say* to the Red Queen, even though you ca'n't help thinking them; and so she trotted on by the Queen's side in silence until they came to a beautiful glade in the wood.

"This," said the Queen, "is our Opening, and I hope," she added, "you'll take advantage of it."

In the middle of the glade, or opening, as the Queen called it, was spread a large White Ensign, which seemed to be intended as the table-cloth and which was covered with all sorts of dishes.

"Now, child," said the Queen, "bustle about and make yourself useful, and we'll have an Imperial picnic."

"But where are all the others?" asked Clara in great surprise. For, though there was plenty to eat for a great many people, she and the Queen were quite by themselves.

"Well," replied the Queen, "I *did* hope some of the others would have come, but I'm not altogether surprised they haven't. They're not yet educated up to a purely Fiscal diet.

"You see," she went on, "the White King and Queen have too much to do with their own quarrels; besides, they wo'n't come out of that precious Tabernacle of theirs; the Red King ca'n't be bothered with Imperial picnics; the Walrus and the Carpenter belong to an anti-picnic league; the Black Knight's exploded; and I suppose the White one has got stuck in some ditch or other on the way. He generally does. Most of the others, I expect, ca'n't manage to get over the fence."

Clara thought it was a very dull sort of picnic. However, as she really felt quite hungry after all the adventures of the day, and as the things on the table-cloth looked very good, she determined to say nothing, and sat down opposite the Queen.

"'I've ordered music," said the Queen; and Clara was conscious of the beating of drums somewhere in the wood near them.

She looked round to see where the sound came from, but it seemed to be all around them, and for a long time Clara could not make out what caused it. Presently, however, she saw what seemed to be the ghost of the Constituent, with what looked like a great drumstick in his hand, flitting in and out

The Picnic

among the trees, and she guessed that it must be he who was responsible for the noise.

"Then I must have killed him when I made him fall from the window," said Clara to herself, "and his ghost has come to haunt me." The thought of this quite took away her appetite, and the picnic seemed duller than ever.

All this time the Queen had been busily inspecting the dishes in front of her; and at last she took up a loaf, and said, "Bread, my dear?"

"Please," said Clara. "At least," she added, hastily, "if that's the Big Loaf you've got before you. Aunt Sarum told me I must never touch the Little One. She said it wouldn't agree with me."

"You don't suppose I'd have anything to do with the Little Loaf; do you?" replied the Queen, rather angrily. "It's too stale." And she began to divide the bread in front of her.

The curious thing was, that the more she cut off the Loaf the bigger it seemed to grow.

"That's always the way, she said, with this Canadian bread—the more you take the more there is, and it gets cheaper instead of dearer, too."

"How *very* peculiar!" said Clara.

"It's a question of supply and demand, child," said the Queen, "which you ca'n't be expected to understand;" and

Clara who had begun to nibble at the piece the Queen had given her, thought the whole thing very dry.

"I know what you'd like," remarked the Queen, suddenly. "You'd like some of this Jugged Rabbit—it's Australian."

"Who jugged it?" asked Clara, rather doubtfully.

"Well, as a matter of fact, it jugged itself," answered the Queen. "But I take credit for the gravy. I made it all myself."

Clara didn't much fancy the look of the Jugged Rabbit, who, on its part, eyed her with an expression of unconcealed dislike.

"You'd better take me as I am," it said at last, after a long pause.

"How dreadfully sociable—no, I mean socialistic," said Clara to the Queen. "I really ca'n't eat food that *talks*."

"It may be socialistic," admitted the Red Queen, "but it's loyal, and that's the great thing after all."

As she spoke, the sound of the drums seemed to get nearer, and Clara began to be quite alarmed.

For a long time the Queen sat and looked at her without speaking in a way Clara didn't at all like, while the sound of drums grew louder and louder.

"Perhaps," she said at last, "you'd prefer some of this Sprigg Chicken," pointing to a Stuffed Peacock as she spoke.

"Certainly not!" replied Clara, with a sudden flicker of determination. "I don't like Sprigg Chicken *at all*."

"Quite right, child," said the Queen. "I don't like it myself, really; but as I invented the dish I have to put up with it, and as you have said 'Ditto' to me, I expect you to pretend to like it too."

To Clara's astonishment, and before she could answer a word, the Stuffed Peacock got up with its nose in the air, walked off the dish, and disappeared into the dark wood.

"Where's it gone to?" asked Clara, who was sorry to lose such a handsome table ornament.

"Oh! It's only gone into Bondage," said the Red Queen, unconcernedly. "It's the natural place for it just now."

"What is Bondage?" asked Clara.

"Why, Afrikander venal servitude, with coat-turning for life, of course" said the Queen. "You've heard of things being in bond, haven't you?"

"Yes," answered Clara, quite sure that she was right this time. "It means that you ca'n't take them out without paying lots and lots of money."

"Exactly," said the Queen, "and *I'm* not going to pay anything at all to get the Stuffed Peacock out."

Clara noticed that the sound of drums had ceased during all the time that they were talking about the Peacock. Now they began again louder than ever.

"But all this time," said the Queen to Clara, "you're getting nothing. Let me introduce you to this beautiful Leg of New Zealand Mutton."

The Picnic

"I'd much rather not, if you don't mind," said Clara (here the sound of the drums became almost deafening). "It looks so tough, you know."

But the Queen only growled: "Clara—Mutton. Mutton—Clara."

"Oh!" said Clara. "This is so seddon."

However, the Leg of Mutton was before her, and she thought they would get nothing to eat at all if things went on as they were doing, so she determined to cut the Mutton whatever happened.

No sooner, however, did she try than the Mutton got up in the dish and glared at her in a way that was positively terrifying.

"I have sent," said the Mutton, in a voice of the deepest reproach, "a fifth and a sixth contingent, and I was ready to send a tenth. And now you want to cut me in favour of that Argentine rubbish."

Clara could only gasp, for the sound of the drums was getting so near that she could hardly manage to think.

"You may have your knife into me," went on the Mutton, "but you ca'n't cut me;" and the Queen said, "Really, Clara, I'm surprised at you. You're enough to spoil anything."

Then all sorts of things began to happen. Thousands of drums appeared in the air all round them, beaten by invisible drummers, while the ghost of the Constituent led this terrible orchestra on the biggest of big drums that Clara had ever seen. The crown on Clara's head gradually loosened itself and floated away in the air, though it still hovered near her.

She felt she was shrinking to her proper size; and at last she grew so giddy and confused with all the noise and turmoil that she threw herself on the ground at the Red Queen's feet.

The Queen stood over her with a sardonic smile upon her lips.

"Shall I ever manage," she said, "to wake her up?"

Chapter XIII

Shaken

The Red Queen took Clara up from the ground and shook her. "I wonder," she said, "whether there's *anything* in the child?"

The drums sounded muffled now. Evidently the ghost of the Constituent thought that he had frightened poor Clara enough.

The Queen shook her harder and harder until Clara's teeth rattled in her head. But it seemed to agree with her, for she kept growing shorter—and fatter—and softer—and rounder—until——

Chapter XIV

Taken

———the Red Queen saw that Clara was only a little kitten after all.

"I *thought* she was," said the Red Queen triumphantly, catching hold of the ribbon round the kitten's neck. "Come along, dear, into the House. I think I'll call you 'Leda'.

And the kitten purred, "Ditto."

Also available from Evertype

Alice's Adventures in Wonderland, 2008

Through the Looking-Glass and What Alice Found There 2009

Wonderland Revisited and the Games Alice Played There
by Keith Sheppard, 2009

A New Alice in the Old Wonderland
by Anna Matlack Richards, 2009

Alice's Adventures under Ground, 2009

The Nursery "Alice", 2010

The Hunting of the Snark, 2010

Alice's Adventures in Wonderland in words of one syllable
retold by Mrs J. C. Gorham, 2010

Eachtraí Eilíse i dTír na nIontas, *Alice* in Irish, 2007

Lastall den Scáthán agus a bhFuair Eilís Ann Roimpi
Looking-Glass in Irish, 2009

Alys in Pow an Anethow, *Alice* in Cornish, 2009

La Aventuroj de Alicio en Mirlando, *Alice* in Esperanto, 2009

Aventures d'Alice au pays des merveilles, *Alice* in French, 2010

Alice's Abenteuer im Wunderland, *Alice* in German, 2010

Anturiaethau Alys yng Ngwlad Hud, *Alice* in Welsh, 2010

www.ingramcontent.com/pod-product-compliance
Lightning Source LLC
Chambersburg PA
CBHW030001050426
42451CB00006B/81